T0146686

MOOD
SWING

MOOD SWING

21 DAYS TO PEACE, JOY & FREEDOM OF MIND

Evelyn Danielle Butler

authorHOUSE®

AuthorHouse™ LLC
1663 Liberty Drive
Bloomington, IN 47403
www.authorhouse.com
Phone: 1-800-839-8640

Published by AuthorHouse   09/30/2014

ISBN: 978-1-4969-4311-8 (sc)
ISBN: 978-1-4969-4312-5 (e)

CONTENTS

DEDICATION

This book is dedicated to my siblings Domanice, Joshulyn, LaKeca, Torrence, and Fallon. May the love, peace and joy of God envelope you all the days of your life.

Acknowledgments

To my loving husband, Brandon, and our legacy, Zoe, thank you for sharing me with the world. I love you.

To my family and friends, I appreciate your acceptance of my transparency and journey. Your support has been unmatched, and I'm grateful for you all.

INTRODUCTION

I wasn't quite sure where to begin or really how to approach this project. Writing a book, much less a devotional, about depression and mental illness proved to be a daunting task. As with many other projects I started working with great momentum and then stopped to talk myself out of finishing. A number of hurdling questions began to rise in my mind: What would my family say? What would my friends think? How would people respond? I was allowing the stigma associated with mental illness to suffocate me into silence. Along with being concerned with my image, I was consumed with thoughts about what qualified me to write such a book. My response to all of the questions and doubts is simple: God graced me to survive. I'm obligated to share His goodness.

I've struggled with self-image. I've experienced loss. I've been in the dark place of depression for reasons unknown. And with each experience, I've seen the light of God's love toward me.

After a short lifetime of gray experiences and more than three years of start/stop writing, I've finally come to the point of being bold enough to share my journey and hopefully lead others out of their tunnels of darkness. Rest assured there is daylight at the end; we just have to pace ourselves and travel carefully.

Before we continue, I want to be clear. I am in no way discouraging you from seeking counsel, nor encouraging you to drop any current treatment plan. Instead this is more of a supplement, offering a 21-day dose of spiritual nourishment, designed to strengthen you on Your journey.

THE BEGINNING

There are a number of myths associated with mental illness but God truly has the last word. On the rare occasions when depression is dealt with in the church, speakers often use the familiar story of Job, citing his miserable story of losing everything. However, God has given us much more encouragement than just Job's story. The Bible is full of references indicating that the wars of the mind and emotions (countenance) are among the oldest and toughest battles to be fought. In truth, the war on the mind began in the garden not long after the beginning of time.

Eve

> *Now the serpent was more cunning than any beast of the field which the Lord God had made. And he said to the woman, "Has God indeed said, 'You shall not eat of every tree of the garden'?" And the woman said*

> *to the serpent, "We may eat the fruit of the trees of the garden' but of the fruit of the tree which is in the midst of the garden, God has said, 'You shall not eat it, nor shall You touch it, lest You die.'" Then the serpent said to the woman, "You will not surely die. For God knows that in the day You eat of it Your eyes will be opened and You will be like God, knowing good and evil." (Gen. 3:1-5)*

Eve was deceived by the serpent leading her to believe that eating of the fruit would surely not cause her to die, instead she'd become wiser knowing the difference between good and evil (Gen. 3). I find it interesting that the word "cunning" is used to describe the serpent. Cunning can be defined as ingenious skill used in a sly or subtle manner. Ingenious has to do with intelligence, and when something is subtle it is difficult to perceive or understand. Depression is a prolonged sadness that can't be warranted by objective reasoning. In other words, it is difficult to understand using typical intelligence; depression is cunning.

Cain

> Not long after Eve's initial encounter, her son, Cain, experienced a mental slump of his own: *but He did not respect Cain and his offering. And Cain was very angry, and his countenance fell.* (Gen. 4:5). Countenance is defined by Merriam-Webster online as calm expression and mental composure. When Cain's countenance fell, he was so beyond his mental boundaries that he killed his own brother. Another theorist may even argue that Cain's mental instability was inherited from his mother who failed

to put protective boundaries in place to keep her mind from being manipulated.

So as you can see, this war has been taking place for a very long time. But there is hope! Not only does His word contain accounts of these journeys, it also contains promises of the good to come. Jeremiah 29:11 says it best: *For I know the thoughts that I think toward you, says the LORD, thoughts of peace and not of evil, to give you a future and a hope.* Because God's word will endure until the ends of the earth, it is with great faith and assurance that I can encourage you.

HELP IS ACCEPTABLE

In many circles, seeking outside help for depression and mental illness is not socially acceptable. In fact, many people avoid seeking help for fear of what others will think or say. However, I have found that many successful people regularly see a mental health professional as they encounter new levels of success. A Biblical example of this can be found in the story of King Saul.

King Saul & David

King Saul struggled with tormenting of the mind, *Now the spirit of the Lord had departed from Saul, and an evil spirit from the Lord tormented him* (1 Sam 16:14). Now imagine that, not only did King Saul struggle with a battle of the mind, it was sent from the Lord! Beyond just having a bad mood, the king was tormented. Torment is associated with ongoing, mental suffering. King Saul's bad mood was such that he even sent out in search of one who could make him feel better, an outside specialist. David was a shepherd and musician with the ability to create a sound that could uplift the mood of the king and silence the evil spirit within him.

As we continue to strive for growth in our personal and spiritual lives, we will undoubtedly encounter more problems. However, the outcome of our success ultimately depends on our response to the problems. Many experts would suggest that in order to be successful, we should mirror the behavior and actions of successful people. Since an ancient and powerful king was wise enough to seek out someone to assist him, why would we, mere average people make the mistake of trying to tackle these problems alone? As you learn more about my journey to wholeness, I encourage you not to go it alone in your personal journey. Seek the companion of a trusted advisor, accountability partner or great counselor to walk alongside you.

My Journey

Before we embark on this voyage together, I want to share some of my personal journey with you. It is my hope that my transparency will allow you to be completely honest and unashamed about your experiences.

Dirty Word

Depression is not an event that occurs overnight. In fact, it can probably be more accurately described as a mold growing in your basement. By the time You see and recognize it, the mold is in your wall! You're fighting like crazy to keep your guests from noticing it until You can have the damage treated. Unfortunately, the distinguished fragrance is undeniable; it's noticeable without anyone actually entering the room. That is how I was, only my odor was that of sorrow. A couple of people were bold enough to call me on it; however, my response was, "I'm fine, just having a bad day." Not only were my bad days much deeper, they were becoming much more regular.

Taboo

As a Young adult, I found myself plagued with an overwhelming sense of sadness that seemed to have accompanied me since childhood. Being an African-American Christian, I found myself twice on the taboo side of emotion. African-Americans for years "didn't do therapy", "depression", or "mental illness". Beyond that, I'd never heard depression talked about in the church, though from my perspective it seemed to be quite prevalent. You had Your issues, laid them on the altar, let go and let God.

My family kept secrets as a means of what they considered to be protection. But really it was paralysis. By not being honest, especially with each other, about our experiences, we were paralyzed from living freely. No one talked about mental illness, though it was evident that many members were battling with some level of mental turmoil. A number of women in my family have suffered from depression, while several of the men have struggled with manic depression and schizophrenia. Yet, not one person was talking openly about it! Instead they allowed alcohol and drugs to fill the voids they were avoiding.

On the Carousel

Between the ages of 5 and 8, a lot of change was happening to and around me. My maternal grandmother, who was a prominent fixture in my life, passed from cancer complications. My mother remarried creating a blended family that involved three other children. We moved to a new setting and transitioned into tighter living arrangements. Than, I learned that I was getting a new sibling. It was as though I was on a carousel of emotion. Death brought sadness and mourning. Remarriage brought a sense of renewed hope. Blended siblings brought a desperate desire to be loved and accepted. Siblings also meant sharing Mommy's love and attention which was all previously directed towards me. Moving demanded losing my own bedroom with full-size bed to a shared bedroom with twin sized accommodations. A new school forced me to feel pressure to fit-in and become a part of my new surroundings. Gaining a new sibling left me once again as the odd-man out, the only person in the house with a different last name. Within 3 years I'd experienced multiple life-altering changes that would be difficult for any child to process on a one-by-one basis, let alone happening back-to-back. My new school didn't have the creative outlets that my previous school offered. My new home didn't allow me to have personal space to claim as my own. My response? Withdrawal. I began to retreat from a vibrant child into a dull wall-flower. That was just the beginning of my journey to blue.

Adolescent Anguish

By the time I entered adolescence, I'd seen and been through quite a bit. I'd observed a close family member's encounters with alcoholism, witnessed domestic violence, been by-stander to other abusive situations and was bullied at school and at home. Around the same time, I became increasingly aware of the gap that was growing between me and my biological father. The pressure was piling up internally; I wasn't coping too well. I often found myself going back and forth in my feelings between depression and anger. But I didn't know how, or with whom, to share all of this with.

As an adolescent experiencing "mood swings", I was initially afraid to admit what I was going through to anyone. My father had been diagnosed with paranoid schizophrenia, and I was concerned that someone would tell me it was hereditary. In a society in which mental illness is overlooked or frowned upon (shunned is probably a better word), I grappled with how honest I should be with myself and others about my father's disease and the impact it had on my life. I later remember having a brief conversation with my older sister inquiring as to whether she was experiencing any difficulties or fears surrounding her mind. We didn't go in depth but we did voice our concerns about the possibility of the illness being generational.

College Confidence

I'd often joked as an adolescent about needing and seeing a therapist of some sort, but no one really took me seriously. Instead, I was sent to church elders, reminded to pray and urged to write down my feelings. When I went off to college, mental health services were available at little to no cost to students on campus. I signed up, leaping at the opportunity for someone to hear my voice! Something didn't feel right. I eventually stopped going. I stopped before making a true connection or experiencing breakthrough. Soon thereafter my closest aunt was diagnosed with breast cancer. I begin feeling an inner turmoil and anxiety about her diagnosis, treatment and outcome. I was a scared 5 year old again.

Mommy

Shortly after my aunt's triumph my mother revealed that she'd been diagnosed with breast cancer and was receiving treatment as well. Her request was that we did not share this information with anyone else as she did not want to damage their faith. Can You imagine the type of pressure holding a secret of this magnitude can cause inside of a person? I was in over my head and wrestling against my own thoughts. "My grandmother was near 40 when she was diagnosed, my aunt 40 and now my mom at 40…My life is going to be over at 40." I experienced the normal (whatever that means) course of emotions and sadness that is expected when a loved one is dealing with this type of disease. But my mind's valley seemed to be deeper than what was considered acceptable.

I went back and forth with the notion of having children; it was a catch-22 for me. Having a child meant that I would essentially leave them early in their lives because I would be ill, but if I started young, I could see them through their teen years. I could do it, but I'd be doing it out of wedlock and for selfish reasons. It wouldn't be fair – but I'd experience the joy of motherhood. Then there was the idea of not having children at all. I didn't want them to experience hurt and loss at this level.

Following the seesaw of family planning related concerns, my mind began deliberations about the physical implications of breast cancer's presence in our family lineage. Could I avert the disease's advantage over me by undergoing a double-mastectomy? If I made such a drastic physical change, would any man understand and be willing to marry me any way? What would people say and think? As you can see, my mind was swirling in several directions. I was focused on all of the wrong things, and I honestly couldn't help myself.

I began to throw myself into work as an escape from the plagues of life. I found it easier to have the excuse of "I have to work" instead of engaging and facing the realities of life. As I continued working, I built a material empire of meaningless things that would help me look the part of having it all together. Just in case I didn't get to live a full life, I wanted career achievements and stuff to show as accomplishments.

Hand Grenade

As if life wasn't already complicated enough, a hand grenade was thrown in my path, totally wrecking my life's perspective. My mother's prognosis had gone from good to great and quickly spiraled into bleak. Her demise actually happened over a matter of days. Just days after sharing the news and new treatment plan, she was admitted to hospice and passed two days later. Now you want to talk about someone being totally wiped out?! I went back to work two days after her burial and acted as though nothing had changed. I withdrew emotionally, but was happy to throw money, glitz and glamour at any situation to make it shine. Not until recently did I realize that I wasn't really living anymore; I was simply existing. But that's another journey, another book…

It took months for the burn-out to catch up with me. But when everything finally came down, it came down hard! I wasn't sleeping; I was barely eating; and I was virtually drowning in sorrow. I knew the jig was up when I was lying naked on the floor of my beautifully decorated townhouse wishing that I could be with my mother on the other side of physical life. I was too fearful to try to commit suicide, but I wished for death to envelope me and end the turmoil. I called a friend and asked her to just talk to me until I fell asleep and she knew something was wrong. She immediately called for backup. With the help of some close family, friends and a great therapist, I was on the road to recovery. At the age of 24, I found myself on an anti-depressant, seeing a therapist and journaling again. I was rebuilding the pieces that had fallen apart.

Unbelievable

In October of the same year, we celebrated 5 years of remission for my aunt. 5 years is "the" mark of freedom in many cancer stories. So as you can imagine, it was incredible to witness her journey and share in her victory. A Christmas proposal from my husband had me convinced that my life was taking a wonderful turn. That is until my aunt revealed that the cancer had returned. This time, the treatment would be far more aggressive and extensive surgery would be required. Please God, not again. How unbelievable that we'd experienced such amazing life highs only to be dropped so low all in a matter of weeks. And that we'd probably drop even further over the next few weeks. Though I took a more involved approach with my aunt, I still buried myself in excuses and busyness. By God's grace, my aunt recovered well, and I didn't completely lose my mind!

Wedding Bells

Just before getting married, I decided against continuing the anti-depressant. I no longer felt creative and free-spirited. I wanted to feel every moment and emotion associated with the process of getting married and fully experience the roller coaster of life itself. Soon my individual therapy turned into couple's therapy, and then simmered to complete nonexistence. Several months later I was back in therapy-different therapist, completely different approach. By the third or fourth session, I'd made up in my mind that it was pretty much a waste of time. I was tired of seeking man's opinion and approval to lift me out of my canyon. "Dear God, take depression away from me as only You can. Have Your way. Set me free. Deliver me.", I prayed. I'd finally reached the point of recognizing that depression wasn't something that you could just treat, it would take true deliverance. I didn't know how or when it was going to happen, but I had the faith to believe that eventually it would. None of it happened overnight; instead, deliverance was a process. What You are reading is a part of my process. I've since come to believe that maintaining deliverance is not only a process, but a daily choice that only I can make.

First Love

When my husband and I decided we were ready for children, we thought it'd be an easy process. But for us, it didn't quite work out that way. After several months of effort we found ourselves pregnant. I was overjoyed knowing that "something wasn't wrong with us". When I realized that we were losing the baby, I was so confused; I couldn't decide whether anger or sadness was the most appropriate response. My confusion led me to being unable to verbalize my thoughts and feelings, eventually causing a build up of emotion. I internalized a lot, played the blame game, guilt game and found myself succumbing to the daze of depression again. How could the loss of someone I'd never met cause me so much heartache? This was a new level of grief that I wasn't equipped to handle. My coping strategies this time? Writing, Crying, Shopping, Repeat.

Rainbow Baby with Dark Clouds

After our miscarriage, it took us nearly a year to conceive again. I was jaded from the first experience so my excitement wasn't near the height that I imagined. I was nervous, cautious, and afraid. I allowed my fear to hold me back from savoring some of the incredible memories that were being made. My labor was complicated so my mind again began to sway and bend under the pressure. By the time our daughter arrived, I was exhausted from being so worried. The exhaustion turned into a greater sense of sadness and disappointment when my plan to nurse our daughter through her first year of life failed miserably. I wasn't eating right, and I certainly wasn't sleeping. Simply put, I was overwhelmed. As a result, she wasn't getting what she needed from me. After a month of toiling, I decided to stop nursing – cold turkey. And the dim place I was in suddenly got darker. I felt like a failure as a mother. In my mind, the one thing that *only I* could do for her was nurse and the connection was lost. My closest circle of friends didn't have children so I didn't feel connected to them either. Life as I knew it changed seemingly over night, and I didn't adapt very well to the new break of day. After a few months of deliberation, I decided that I owed my family a better me. I spent time talking with my doctors and chose an anti-depressant to assist with the challenges I faced.

Another Loss

Just when I thought I had a solid grasp and good footing on life's mountain, the cord snapped again. My missing father had been found deceased and it was likely related to his mental illness. I was hundreds of miles away trying to process the unbelievable chain of events that led up to the phone call. I spent hours and days on the phone coordinating the details of my father's home-going with strangers, both familial and literal. The morning of his services I woke up with the intention of numbing myself to the emotion of it all. I stared blankly during the service as those around me mourned the loss of our loved one. It was later that I finally allowed myself to grieve – my thought "I am an adult orphan." So there I was feeling under myself. Yes, you read that right, I was under myself not just down on myself. I'd lost my first child and both of my parents. I was a TOTAL wreck! I had to take a moment and walk my own path, AGAIN.

Here & Now

It's been said that experience makes an expert. So now I've been through all these things, and a few more not even mentioned here. I guess I'm more qualified to share on depression than I thought I was. My experiences may not be as extreme as yours, or perhaps You couldn't even imagine some of these things. Regardless of where we fit on the spectrum of "oh that's so sad", the truth is that we all deserve to move forward towards wholeness. That's why I'm here now seeing this book through to completion.

YOUR JOURNEY

I want to share God's joy with you. I've been in the dark place and know the joy of experiencing freedom. After all, His Word says "...Do not sorrow, for the joy of the Lord is Your strength" (Nehemiah 8:10). *Mood Swing* is a 21 day journey to your joy, strength, and freedom. Some days will be easier than others, and some will require you to make a conscious choice to do something different. In fact, your voyage may even last longer than 21 days with you choosing to devote more time to a particular focus. Whatever the length, stay the course and reap the reward. The remaining pages of this book contain scriptures, prayers and encouraging words to meditate on throughout the day. I urge you to write on the pages, highlight the things that resonate with your spirit and document your journey. You deserve to be released from the strongholds. "Therefore if the Son make you free, you shall be free indeed." John 8:36

Gracious Father,

> *I come today on behalf of every reader of this book, simply thanking You for another opportunity to enter into Your throne room, naked and unashamed. I thank You for an opportunity to lay our burdens at*

Your feet with truth and transparency. God it says in Your word that "By His stripes we are healed" (Is. 53:5). I believe that healing goes much deeper than our physical body and extends even to our minds. Lord, You are not a man that You should lie so, today I claim healing in Jesus' name. I plead the blood of Jesus as a hedge of protection around every reader and their families right now. Lord God, as they embark on this journey to wholeness and freedom, I ask that You demonstrate Your unconditional love towards them. Send the Holy Spirit as their comforter and guide. Over the next 21 days, or more, I expect You to move mightily in their lives. Standing on Your word, I call forth transformation by the renewing of their mind. Open their ears so that they might hear You clearly. Give them peace and understanding. Breathe on them Lord. Send Your wind, a fresh anointing, their way. Declaring the victory, I thank You in advance. In Your son Jesus' mighty name we pray. Amen.

Day 1

**And do not seek what you should eat or what you
should drink, nor have an anxious mind.**

Luke 12:29

So it's day 1 and you're wondering how this is all going to
shake down. In fact, you may even be anxious because this
may be your last resort. You've tried everything else and
just want true relief. As you go through today, ask God to
remove all anxiety associated with your new journey. Trust
God to provide everything that you need in this season.

Lord God,

*Thank You for giving me the courage to take the next step.
Please settle my heart and remove all anxiety. I trust You to
provide everything that I need in this season. Let me not worry
about "if" I will overcome. Instead, allow me to praise You in
advance of "when" I overcome. In Jesus' precious name, Amen.*

Day 2

***Why are you cast down, O my soul? And why are
you disquieted within me? Hope in God, for I shall
yet praise Him for the help of His countenances***

Psalms 42:5

By the time You recognize and acknowledge that you are
suffering from depression, you usually can't remember where
it all actually began. Seek God today on the root cause of
your current battle. How can we strategize and fight unless
we know our enemy?

Heavenly Father,

*Thank You for showing up as a light in my life. God cause Your
light to shine even in the dark recesses of my heart. Reveal the
true cause of my sadness and bitterness. Show me the people
that I need to forgive. Show me where I need to release guilt
and forgive myself. Allow me to experience the fullness of Your
countenance and express my contentment through praise. In
Jesus' name I pray. Amen.*

_____
_____
_____
_____
_____
_____
_____
_____
_____
_____
_____
_____
_____
_____
_____
_____
_____
_____
_____
_____
_____
_____

Day 3

**As iron sharpens iron, So a man sharpens
the countenance of his friend.**

Proverbs 27:17

As you embark on this journey, it is necessary that you get some people in your life that can sharpen you. It's time to take inventory of the people you have in your life. If they are accompanying your misery (since they say misery loves company), let them go. Ask God today to strategically rearrange the inhabitants of your inner circle.

Heavenly Father,

Thank You for giving me the courage to continue on this journey with You. Help me to rearrange the relationships in my life during this time. I want to be sharpened. In Jesus' name I pray. Amen.

_____

_____

_____

_____

_____

_____

_____

_____

_____

_____

_____

_____

_____

_____

_____

_____

_____

_____

_____

_____

Day 4

Lift up Your heads, O you gates, And be lifted up, you everlasting doors! And the King of glory shall come in.

Psalms 24:7

When we have walked under the weight of depression and other mental challenges, our head is often downcast. Though we are at the beginning of this journey, it is time to lift our heads. Prepare the way for the King of Glory to come.

Dear Heavenly Father,

Today I lift my head towards You. I raise my head as a symbol of invitation for You to come in and have complete reign in my life. I thank You Lord that even on my bad days, You remind me that the purpose of lifting my head and opening the doors is so that You may be glorified. Your word says that if You be lifted up, You will draw all men unto You. So today, as I lift my head, I am choosing to honor You. I am being drawn closer to You, and I thank You for the intimacy. In Jesus' name. Amen.

Day 5

**Create in me a clean heart, O God, and
renew a steadfast spirit within me.**

Psalms 51:10

Sometimes we experience so much that our hearts become
tainted. We carry around emotional baggage that weighs
us down and prevents us from moving at a steady pace
towards freedom and success. Today, ask God to clean your
heart and remove all things that prevent you from moving
towards steadfast progress.

Heavenly Father,

*Show me the things in my heart that are not of You. Cleanse my
heart with the blood of Your son, Jesus. God renew a steadfast
spirit within me. Make me consistent in my demeanor. Allow
me to move forward on this journey with confidence in You. In
Jesus' name, Amen.*

Day 6

And do not be conformed to this world, but be transformed by the renewing of your mind, that you may prove what is that good and acceptable and perfect will of God.

Romans 12:2

The world in which we live is a very complicated and troubled place. Focus your attention today on being transformed. What does transformation look like for you? It starts with thinking differently then following through with actions. Submit your thoughts and actions to the will of God.

Heavenly Father,

Today, I submit my mind and will to You. I ask Lord, that You transform my thoughts so that they are aligned with Your will. Through Your Holy Spirit, make what You want for me become my greatest desire. Allow me to pursue Your good, acceptable and perfect will until my purpose is fulfilled in You. Grant me, O Lord, the strength to resist the thoughts and actions of this world. Instead allow me to only be moved by that which is pleasing unto You. Thank You Lord for not just changing my mind, but totally transforming my mind to operate differently. In Your son's name I pray, Amen.

_____
_____
_____
_____
_____
_____
_____
_____
_____
_____
_____
_____
_____
_____
_____
_____
_____
_____
_____
_____
_____

Day 7

and be renewed in the spirit of your mind

Ephesians 4:23

The word 'renew' means to make new again, indicating that we once had something new to start. Today's focus is again on God making our minds like new, before they were clouded with all of the images and occurrences that have led us to lives of hurt and disappointment.

Dear Lord,

I thank You for making my mind new in You again today. Father, remove the deposits that have caused my mind to become crowded and my spirit to become overwhelmed. Replace my spirit's contents with thoughts of love, joy and goodness as only You can. In Jesus' name I pray, Amen.

_____

_____

_____

_____

_____

_____

_____

_____

_____

_____

_____

_____

_____

_____

_____

_____

_____

_____

_____

_____

Day 8

Let this mind be in you which was also in Christ Jesus

Philippians 2:5

Christ Jesus was a perfect man sent to live in an imperfect world. Yet, He was able to maintain a mindset focused on His purpose. He did not become caught up in the woes and imperfections. Instead, He responded to every situation with love and compassion. He fulfilled his work despite his circumstances. Today's thought is on maintaining a Christ-like mind in the midst of your circumstances and surroundings.

Lord Jesus,

Today my heart's desire is for a mind like Yours. I am determined to move forward in my destiny, not allowing for distractions or delays to rise in my mind. Teach me how to think like You. I thank You for a new mentality. In Your name I pray, Amen.

_____

_____

_____

_____

_____

_____

_____

_____

_____

_____

_____

_____

_____

_____

_____

_____

_____

_____

_____

_____

Day 9

**Jesus said unto him, "You shall love the
Lord your God with all your heart, with all
your soul, and with all your mind."**

Matthew 22:37

Today focus on loving the Lord with everything that is in you. As you purpose to love Him with your whole mind, no room is left for any other intrusion or distractions. You can only think one thought at a time; make it a good one surrounded by love. Let your love for Him drive your thoughts throughout the day. You might be surprised at the change in perspective.

Lord God,

Today I choose to focus on loving You with all of me. God, I empty my heart and refill it with thoughts of You. Touch my mind, O' Lord, so that I am constantly reminded of Your goodness. Thank You that as I focus on You, everything else is wiped away. I love You Lord. In Jesus' name, Amen.

Day 10

Commit your works to the Lord, And your thoughts will be established

Proverbs 16:3

Many times we go about our daily work and tasks for a pay check or recognition, or because "somebody's gotta do it". Yesterday we focused on our thoughts. Today, turn over your efforts and actions to the Lord. Observe how your attitude and emotions are impacted by having a different focus and total alignment.

Gracious Lord,

I thank You for another opportunity to exercise my mind and limbs in work. I give all of my efforts over to You and perform tasks with You in mind. I thank You Lord for the organizing and firming of my thoughts. Thank You for a new foundation for my thoughts. In Jesus' name I pray, Amen.

Day 11

**Therefore we do not lose heart. Even though
our outward man is perishing, yet the inward
man is being renewed day by day.**

2 Corinthians 4:16

We've hit the midpoint of our journey! Some days may have
been better than others. However, I do not want you to lose
heart. Mind renewal is a daily process. Focus on the renewal
that takes place on today. Tomorrow do the same. Take this
journey day-by-day.

Heavenly Father,

*My commitment to this journey has not been easy. However,
my trust and hope in You is greater than the difficulty. Today,
I ask that Your Holy Spirit continue to encourage me. Allow me
not to lose heart. Instead, grant me daily renewal of my spirit.
In Jesus' mighty name I pray, Amen.*

———————————————————————————
———————————————————————————
———————————————————————————
———————————————————————————
———————————————————————————
———————————————————————————
———————————————————————————
———————————————————————————
———————————————————————————
———————————————————————————
———————————————————————————
———————————————————————————
———————————————————————————
———————————————————————————
———————————————————————————
———————————————————————————
———————————————————————————
———————————————————————————
———————————————————————————
———————————————————————————
———————————————————————————
———————————————————————————

Day 12

A merry heart makes a cheerful countenance,
But by sorrow of the heart the spirit is broken.

Proverbs 15:13

A cheerful disposition begins in the heart. Often times we carry hurts and disappointments that build into calluses of sorrow in our hearts. Make a conscious decision to acknowledge and remove even the hidden weights. Today we will reclaim a merry heart and repair our broken spirits.

Dear Lord,

I pour out the contents of my heart before You today. I lay all of my sorrow at Your feet and invite You to repair the broken places of my spirit. I thank You Lord for happiness residing in my heart and overtaking my disposition. I thank You Lord for a cheerful countenance moving forward. In Jesus' name, Amen.

_____

_____

_____

_____

_____

_____

_____

_____

_____

_____

_____

_____

_____

_____

_____

_____

_____

_____

_____

_____

_____

_____

Day 13

He who has knowledge spares his words,
And a man of understanding is of a calm spirit.

Proverbs 17:27

Sometimes we enter into situations and totally lose it. We fly off the handle unleashing the wrath of our tongues. Long after it's over we find our selves still bothered by the occurrence. Today, focus on sparing your words and gaining understanding of situations. Be proactive instead of reactive. I expect that your posture of proactive understanding will allow things that once troubled you to be a nonfactor. Instead, your preparation will bring you a calm confidence.

Heavenly Father,

Today I ask for a spirit of knowledge and understanding. With the guidance of Your Holy Spirit, I know that I am able to live with a calm spirit. I accept the calm spirit that You have offered. I embrace the peace that a calm spirit brings in every area of my life. In Jesus' name, Amen.

_____

_____

_____

_____

_____

_____

_____

_____

_____

_____

_____

_____

_____

_____

_____

_____

_____

_____

_____

_____

_____

Day 14

A man has joy by the answer of his mouth,
And a word spoken in due season, how good it is!

Proverbs 15:23

It is easy to fall into the "I'm doing okay" routine, imploring people to dig deeper: "Are you sure?" or "What's really going on?" Today, obtain your joy by speaking it. Focus on the good. Say something different. Share your joy by extending a positive word to someone else.

Lord God,

Rearrange the words of my mouth to reflect the joyful contents of my heart. As I speak with joy given by You, permit me to share a word in due season with someone else. Let me be a carrier of good through my mouth. Focus my mind on Your joy so that I may be a light to myself and among others. In Jesus' name I pray. Amen.

_____

_____

_____

_____

_____

_____

_____

_____

_____

_____

_____

_____

_____

_____

_____

_____

_____

_____

_____

_____

_____

_____

_____

Day 15

**The LORD lift up His countenance upon you,
And give you peace.**

Numbers 6:26

Let's face it, some days we just don't feel like it. On those days it's important to go a step further than "God give me a cheerful countenance"; we have to activate, "Lord, give me YOUR countenance". His countenance is joined by peace in our lives. With His countenance upon us, we avoid the perils of just not feeling it.

Dear Lord,

Today I ask that You replace my countenance with Yours. Give me Your peace that I may move forward in my purpose. Let Your Holy Spirit lead me past distraction and into Your presence. May I express joy as Your countenance provides peace. In Jesus' name, Amen.

_____

_____

_____

_____

_____

_____

_____

_____

_____

_____

_____

_____

_____

_____

_____

_____

_____

_____

_____

_____

_____

Day 16

**You will keep him in perfect peace,
Whose mind is stayed on You,
Because he trusts in You.**

Isaiah 26:3

Often times on this journey called life, it is easy to get distracted. Whether it's something happening at work, school, home or elsewhere- there are subtle things that can quickly turn our focus off of our destination and goals. Today's exercise is in trusting God and staying focused on His promises to you.

Gracious Lord,

Thank You once again for another opportunity to experience Your grace and mercy. As I emerge today, I declare Your goodness to be my main focus. Allow me to keep Your Word suspended in front of me as a memorial of peace. I thank You Lord that as I keep my mind on You, Lord You will cause me to live a life of perfect peace. I understand that everyday won't be roses, but Your peace will reign supreme. More than that, Lord I trust You. In Jesus' name I pray. Amen.

_____

_____

_____

_____

_____

_____

_____

_____

_____

_____

_____

_____

_____

_____

_____

_____

_____

_____

_____

_____

_____

_____

Day 17

He who heeds the word wisely will find good,
And whoever trusts in the LORD, happy is he.

Proverbs 16:20

Today I urge you to put your trust totally in the Lord. Though times may have seemed troubling, the fact that you're still living is reason enough to trust Him with everything else in your life. As you trust Him more, you will be endowed with happiness.

Gracious Father,

Thank You for Your word that brings wisdom to my life. I appreciate the consistent guidance that Your word offers. As I turn my life over to You, I surrender my all to Your will. I trust You with everything in my world. Thank You Lord for exchanging my worries for Your happiness. I am excited about finding good in my life today! In Jesus' name, Amen.

_____

_____

_____

_____

_____

_____

_____

_____

_____

_____

_____

_____

_____

_____

_____

_____

_____

_____

_____

_____

_____

Day 18

The LORD is my strength and my shield;
My heart trusted in Him, and I am helped;
Therefore my heart greatly rejoices,
And with my song I will praise Him.

Psalms 28:7

Isn't it awesome to know that not only will God strengthen you; He'll protect you too. Once we commit to totally trusting Him our reward is happiness and joy. All the things you have been through are absolutely nothing in comparison to the joy that will be bestowed upon you as You make the choice to trust Him.

Dear Lord,

I thank You for being my strength and shield during this journey. I am grateful for the opportunity to learn to trust You more and more. Thank You Heavenly Father for helping me. God I thank You for restoring joy to my life. I will sing of Your goodness and my gratefulness. I appreciate Your joy reigning (and raining) in my life. You are an awesome God! In Jesus' name, Amen.

Day 19

I will greatly rejoice in the LORD,
My soul shall be joyful in my God;
For He has clothed me with the garments of salvation,
He has covered me with the robe of righteousness,
As a bridegroom decks himself with ornaments,
And as a bride adorns herself with her jewels.

Isaiah 61:10

When we get new clothes, we always feel better. How great do you feel in knowing that God has replaced your robes of depression, bitterness and anger with salvation, righteousness and jewels? Take delight and pleasure today in God and the new found expression you have in Him!

Great God,

My soul rejoices in You today! God I thank You for bringing me to a point that my soul can cry out hallelujah rather than seeping sorrow. God You are magnificent and I exalt Your presence in my life! Lord, I delight in the transformation that You have sparked within me. Thank You for redeeming my expression in You. Thank You for extreme joy and total peace. In Jesus' name, Amen.

Day 20

**Blessed *are* the people who know the joyful sound!
They walk, O LORD, in the light of Your countenance.**

Psalms 89:15

Do you know the sound of joy? Can you remember moments where you've uttered or heard a squeal of delight or shout of triumph? The day has come again! Make a joyful sound today because you have obtained the countenance of the Lord.

Dear Lord,

Thank You! Thank You! Thank You! With my whole heart I will praise You and with my lips I will honor You! I bless Your name O' God for placing the sound of joy in my mouth. Thank You for allowing me to recognize that today I am blessed. My mind is changed for the better in You. I am stronger because of Your joy. In Jesus' name, Amen.

_____
_____
_____
_____
_____
_____
_____
_____
_____
_____
_____
_____
_____
_____
_____
_____
_____
_____
_____
_____
_____
_____
_____

Day 21

**For God has not given us a spirit of fear, but
of power and of love and of a sound mind.**

2 Timothy 1:7

**You will keep *him* in perfect peace,
Whose mind *is* stayed *on You,*
Because he trusts in You.**

Isaiah 26:3

Many times when we set out to embark on a new journey we are met with fear. As we conclude our time together, denounce any remnants of fear and proclaim victory in power and love. Revel in peace, knowing that God has given you a sound mind. Thank God for the work He has done in you. Your freedom and deliverance has come! Walk out deliverance daily. Continue to seek God for his direction and always follow after peace.

Dear Lord,

I thank You for the past 21 days together. I thank You for showing forth Your sovereignty and faithfulness. God I am forever changed by the time took to meet me where I was and usher me into Your presence. I bless Your name for a renewed mind and transformed spirit. Heavenly Father, Your Word declares that You have not given me a spirit of fear, but of power, love and a sound mind. I thank You that as I move closer to my destiny, You send Your angels to clear the path.

Thank You for wiping the obstacle of fear out of my life that I may live fearlessly. Lord, I thank You for my new found power in You. I have experienced Your love and therefore know how to better give and receive love. God, I thank You most of all for providing me with a sound mind, directed by Your precious Holy Spirit. I trust You to handle all of me. I give You the glory, praise, and honor for my victory in You. In Jesus' matchless name I pray. Amen

Evelyn Danielle Butler

_____

_____

_____

_____

_____

_____

_____

_____

_____

_____

_____

_____

_____

_____

_____

_____

_____

_____

_____

Closing

As we conclude our time together, it is my prayer that you have been encouraged to push beyond the restraints and pressures of your mind. You now have an arsenal of God's word to employ anytime it appears that the enemy is closing in. May you choose daily to walk in your new found joy and freedom. Congratulations on the transformation of your mind! Enjoy the new view from your Mood Swing!

**Grace to you and peace from God our
Father and the Lord Jesus Christ.**

1 Corinthians 1:3